THINK LIKE
A CEO
ACT LIKE A MOM

The Pursuit of Work

&

Life Integration

TAMEIKA ISAAC DEVINE

Table of Contents

olland is a friend, a colleague, and perhaps one
f the best examples of what can happen when a
oman "thinks like a CEO, acts like a Mom!"

Dedication

‿‿‿‿‿‿‿‿‿‿‿‿‿‿‿‿‿‿‿‿‿‿‿‿‿

I give honor to my Lord and Savior, Jesus Christ, who has allowed me to live this incredible life. He has granted me the blessing of being a mother and for that I am eternally grateful.

This book is dedicated to the best example of a working mom a girl could have, my mother, Veronica Manigo Isaac. Growing up, my mom showed me how you can excel in your career and be the homeroom mom, girl scout troop leader and band chaperone. She made managing a career and household look easy (I now know it is not) and inspired me to be a great mom without sacrificing my own personal dreams and aspirations. To this day, she is still my shero and I would not be the woman I am today without her example.

To Tamia, Jade and Jameson, I wake up everyday with joy and gratitude in my heart for being able to have the awesome opportunity of being your mommy. Thank you for understanding late nights, meetings and days away from you. Thank you for always telling me what a great mom I am and recognizing that everything that I do, although not always be directly related to you, is for you.

To my husband, Jamie, without your love and support I could not do all that I do. Thank you for loving me unconditionally and supporting all of my goals and dreams. Thank you for being an amazing father and being a partner in this thing we call parenting.

To my sister circle – you know who you are – thank you for being you and loving me. Thanks for the talks over wine or in the spa, the encouraging text messages and memes and for always lending an ear.

Author's Note

Even in the 21st century, society still prorwomen to believe that mother and vigorous pursuit of professionentrepreneurial aspirations will jeopardize well being of their children and their family As a result, a few women forego marriage a motherhood altogether; many others delay ma and/or motherhood; and many, many mo to *balance* motherhood and family with a profession or business – an exhausting and vi impossible feat. I maintain, in this book, tł most desirable outcome with regard to a w maternal/family life and her career/profes work life is *integration* of the two.

Although not typical of most forewords, that follows provides a powerful example c life *integration* – what women can achiev they refuse to place limits on either thei aspirations or their professional/entrep dreams and instead seek to *integrate* them. L

Foreword

⬩⬩⬩⬩⬩⬩⬩⬩⬩⬩⬩⬩⬩⬩⬩⬩⬩⬩⬩⬩⬩⬩⬩⬩⬩⬩⬩

*G*rowing up, I used to envy the kids who knew what they wanted to be when they grew up. When asked, the kids in my elementary school class would yell out "Fireman," "Astronaut," "Doctor" or whatever their 2nd grade minds thought of. I never knew – at least not at that age. Looking back, I believe I never had an answer because what I wanted to be, I had yet to discover. One thing I was sure of was that I never wanted to be broke. I was blessed to come from a family that showed me financial freedom at a young age. My grandfather would tell me stories of his father, who built Marshalls Corner, the first black-owned grocery store in Charles County, Maryland. My grandfather owned 167 acres and worked his land. He was my first example of the scripture, "Ye shall lend to many nations, but you shall not borrow," given that he was a lender to many people in Charles County. He built the first Negro League baseball diamond in Pomonkey, Maryland; built his home debt free and paid cash for everything. In fact, he financed my first car. Consequently, I knew at an early age, that I didn't want to be broke; I wanted the same kind of financial freedom I saw growing up.

Because I saw my mother create multiple revenue streams, it was natural for me to develop a mindset of using what was in my hand to make money. In high school, I sold hand-designed, custom T-Shirts and did nails in my mother's nail salon. I was an entrepreneur before I even knew the word. In college, I did nails in my dorm room and sold Mary Kay Cosmetics. In fact, entrepreneurship helped me put myself through college. When I got married at the youthful age of 23, my husband and I started a vending machine business. The money we made from this business allowed us to acquire enough money to begin buying real estate. Eventually, we created CEI Motion Real Estate Development Co. The money from the real estate allowed us the opportunity to purchase an asset-based lending brokerage firm, Biz Lending Solutions. Today, we own Holland & Holland Enterprises, Finergy, Inc. and CEI Motion Real Estate Development Company.

I remember that when I was pregnant with my older son, I was sitting in his nursery thinking that I didn't want him to start from ground zero. I wanted to be able to give him a head start in life – I wanted my ceiling to be his floor. My children have grown up watching my husband and me doing business. We never used our kids as an excuse for why we could not do business. When we started the vending machine business, we used to take them to Sam's Club with us and we let them track inventory for the vending machines. At that time, my older son was in the 3rd grade; his brother was in the 2nd grade. If we were meeting with our real estate attorney, the boys were in the office with to help them care for their families in a way that allows them to live phenomenal lives. We MUST take heed to her impartation. Our world is changing rapidly and we must develop the vision, the skillset and the execution to position our families for success.

LaShawne

LaShawne Holland
Global Wealthy Life Architect
America's Wealth Activator
Founder, LaShawne Holland International and
Wealthy Leaders Institute

us, sitting quietly in the corner playing with their Game Boy. When we started Biz Lending Solutions and had board meetings with our business partners, my sons were also at the table, listening. I doubt they understood what was going on, but they were right there with us. We used to play Monopoly with them, so that when we went out to look at properties, they knew that we were buying four green houses so that we could get one big red hotel. We showed them how to play real-life Monopoly!

My grandfather use to say, "What you do in moderation, your kids will grow up to do in excess." I watched my kids develop their own entrepreneurial wings while they were in elementary school - selling snacks on the school bus on the long ride home. So, when the children were 8, 11 and 12 years old, I was not taken by surprise when they wanted to start their own business. My husband and I loaned them the money to start AJ's Hawaiian Iceez - and yes, we charged them interest. They paid us back 100% of our money from their first vending opportunity. In a little over a year, they had made $110,000. Imagine making six figures at 12 and 13 years old! They ordered their supplies from Hawaii, negotiated all of their vending opportunities and hired their friends to work for them in the state-of-the-art shaved ice trailer they purchased. They purchased a pick-up truck when they were too young to have a license! The media heard of their story and the attention they garnered went on and on: they received a letter from President Barack Obama; they won *Black Enterprise Magazine Teenpreneur of the Year*

Award; they won Ernst & Young's Youthpreneur Award; they were the first teenagers ever to speak at the start of the Inc. 500/5000 Annual Conference; they appeared on the pilot of a BET television series. Their early experiences helped them develop an amazing work ethic. Upon graduating from college, my older son took over management of our gourmet, hand-blended tea company, Holland & Holland Enterprises. The company has also just launched Sea Sauce, Inc – a old family recipe for seafood. I am proud of the budding entrepreneur he is. When my younger son graduates from college, he will manage our real estate company; my daughter will manage our foundation.

Building a business empire with my husband has been one of the most amazing experiences I could ever have dreamed of. We are family; we are in this together. As a wife and mother of three, I have worked hard to build a company at which my children can, one day, take the helm. A wise man (or woman) leaves an inheritance to his children's children. So, building a multi-million-dollar enterprise did not just happen - it was intentional. Helping your children discover their gifts, passions and purpose has to be intentional. And because we supported their business early on, my sons registered me to attend an event in Atlanta, GA and my world shifted.

As a result of attending a business branding bootcamp - I thought I was attending to learn something I could use to help my kids with their business - the Wealthy Leaders Institute was born. I had been teaching personal finance at my church for 18+ years for **free**; it was at the business

branding bootcamp that I discovered my calling - the reason I am here on this earth. I had not previously realized that what I was doing could be a profitable business for me. At any rate, in 2011, I began the journey of building a global wealth development company. Simply put, we teach people how to multiply their money.

I feel blessed to be walking out my calling in life. I feel honored to help my kids walk out theirs and to support their vision for financial freedom, financial independence and control of their own destinies. Our business enterprises have allowed us to build an amazing life, provide my kids with a world-class education and allow them the option of not working for anyone else. So, when I hear women say they can't build a business or live their dreams because they have small children, I tell them that that mindset is the voice of scarcity talking. Your children don't prevent you from moving forward, they should motivate you to move forward. Your kids should be your **why** - the very reason why you can't stay stuck.

In working with women leaders, over the years, I have recognized that many of them have the potential to build great businesses and achieve great wealth. However, too many of them subscribe to the idea that they cannot do so because they have a family for which they must care. In the book, Think like a CEO, Act Like a Mom, Tameika shatters that myth. Think Like a CEO, Act Like a Mom describes for women how, with the proper mindset, training and support, they can achieve great professional success and use that professional success

Introduction

For as long as I can remember, I have wanted to be an attorney. In fact, when I was about seven years-old, I received a chalkboard as a gift and, instead of playing school like most kids did, I played court. I would use the chalkboard to diagram things for my dolls and stuffed animals, who were my jury. I had visions of wearing designer suits and walking into court with a fancy briefcase. Although I never "dreamed" of becoming a mom, it was a given. I loved children and having a working mom, I never considered that I could not have an amazing career and be a great mom as well. I saw my mom do it and I knew I would do it, too. And then when The Cosby Show came out, I saw Claire Huxtable. She was smart, beautiful and accomplished. She had an adoring husband, amazing children and a clapback that kept her classy but made it clear that she was not someone to mess with. That was going to be me. The professional woman with the picture perfect home life. No one could tell me that I could not have it all.

After high school, I went on to attend Hampton University, a historically black university, and then on to law school at The University of South Carolina. I was well on my way to the career and life I had planned.

When I got pregnant with my first child at age 32, I was successfully practicing law in my own law firm and serving as an elected member of our city council. Becoming a mom was just a natural part of my life's journey. It was not something that I felt needed to derail, redirect or change my career aspirations. If anything, it further motivated me to continue setting and pursuing big goals. Did I have to change how I did a few things? Of course. But I did not have to sacrifice or minimize my career aspirations by becoming a mom.

For years society has trained women to believe that in order to be great moms, we have to balance, or make equal, our work obligations and our home life. However, work obligations and home life can never be made equal; work-life balance does not exist! Sadly, because we have been taught to strive for this nonexistent balance, we feel that we have failed when we can't achieve it. Like innumerable other women, I chased that imaginary work-life balance for many years. I thought I could be that Enjoli woman – the one that "brought home the bacon, fried it up in a pan and never let my husband forget he's a man." Of course I also had to take children to school, make lunches, do homework, etc. Work-life *balance* was a fantasy destined to disappoint. Then, I had an *A-ha!* moment when I decided to stop trying to achieve work-life *balance* and instead learn to practice work-life *integration*.

"What," you might ask, "is *work-life integration*? Isn't that the same as *work-life balance*?" Actually, it is not. The word "integrate" means "to form, coordinate, or blend into a functioning or unified whole." *Work-life Integration* is the recognition that your work and your personal life can't be separated because they are both part of who you are. Work-life integration focuses on coordinating or blending the different aspects of your life to create a whole picture - a picture of your complete self. In today's fast paced world, it is impractical to believe that you can - and futile to try to - divide yourself into separate entities, equally productive at home and in the workplace, not to mention trying to take care of yourself psychologically, spiritually and mentally. It is better to embrace your complete self and pursue work life integration.

Rather than pushing you to seek some impossible balance between work responsibilities and your personal life, work-life integration encourages you to recognize that a career and a personal life are both significant parts of who you are. The inability to integrate both of these important pieces of yourself leaves you constantly pulled in opposite directions, feeling stressed, overwhelmed and unfulfilled. Work-life integration allows you to figure out what works best for you. It gives you the ability to fully shine as the person you are, without sacrificing a piece of your greatness.

Most people recognize the need to create meaningful engagement among the interconnected roles, relationships and responsibilities in their lives. Yet many are at a loss as to how to create that engagement. This book is designed to share with you the rules to which I adhere in order to achieve work-life integration. In developing the rules, I conducted informal research into, observations of and interactions with successful business leaders in order to identify key principles they applied in creating outstanding business enterprises. I then "translated" or adapted some of these principles into rules that women – in particular – could apply to their lives in order to achieve balance among their myriad roles and responsibilities. Twelve rules are described in the book, with specific examples of their application taken from my own life. Following each rule is *homework* designed to help you begin your own journey toward work-life integration. I hope you will not short change yourself by skipping the exercises; they are critical to helping you achieve the phenomenal life you deserve.

RULE # 1

Operate as the CEO of Your Life

When I decided to run for office, I was a full-time prosecutor with the SC Attorney General's Office. Being a state employee was not ideal for someone who was running for office and needed a lot of flexibility, so I decided to do the only thing I could – become an entrepreneur. I teamed up with two of my friends from law school and we opened our own law firm. I was super excited about the opportunities ahead of me. Growing up as the daughter of an entrepreneur, I've always had an entrepreneurial spirit; I knew that I could be very successful as my own boss. As we planned our own law firm, we worked diligently on the startup: finding office space, filing the necessary incorporation documents, buying furniture, etc. However, in my excitement to start practicing, I did not think about the foundational things that were truly needed to plan for long term success.

After a few years in business, with things going well, I decided to take a business development class. The class was for established business owners and designed to take us back to the basics. The instructors recognized that most business people worked so much "in" their business that they did not work "on" their business. These instructors recognized that if you do not work "on" your business as much as you work "in" your business, you are destined to fail.

Throughout the class we talked about having a mission statement and a vision for our business. The class prompted me to step back from the day-to-day operations of my law business and really examine my long-term goals and how to achieve them. The class also helped me focus on describing my "ideal" customers and what I needed to do to serve them effectively. I worked, at length, on a vision statement for the law firm. I thought about my goals for the practice and how I was going to achieve those goals. I focused on what I wanted my practice to be and, more importantly, what I didn't want it to be.

The class and the process of reflection, visualization and goal setting gave me a better understanding of how important it is to lay the proper foundation for any worthwhile endeavor. I started thinking, "What if I apply these same business principles to my own life?" The point of a vision statement is to describe a desired future position or state of affairs.

The statement expresses our hopes and dreams. Most of us, however, do not engage in a thoughtful systematic process to come up with a vision for our lives and very rarely do we memorialize it on paper.

I considered the process I had employed to create and articulate the vision for my law firm and decided to apply it to my life. For example, I considered how I wanted to show up as a wife and mother; I envisioned what I wanted my professional life to look like; I looked at where I wanted to be spiritually and in my relationships with others. Most importantly, I decided that I was the CEO of my life.

What does being a CEO mean? A CEO is the Chief Executive Officer of a business or organization. The CEO is the person with the ability and the authority to make executive decisions for the organization or business. As CEO of my life, I was responsible for articulating a vision for my life, setting goals for my life and taking full responsibility for my achievements and my failures. Habakkuk 2:2 states, "Write the vision, and make it plain upon tables, that he may run that readeth it." Once I formulated a vision, I wrote it down in my journal. I also put the vision on a *vision board.* Creating a vision board is probably one of the most valuable visualization tools available to you. This powerful tool serves as your image of the future – a tangible representation of where you are going. It represents your dreams, your goals, and your ideal life. Writing the vision in a journal and on a vision board allowed me to the see a physical manifestation of my vision. It also helped me set realistic short-term goals to make the vision a reality.

Are *you* operating as the CEO of your life? As the CEO of your life, you need to set the direction for your life and your household. You have the ability and the authority to make the important decisions. For example:

- You define the vision, mission and goals for your life;
- You are responsible for implementing short and long-term plans;
- You set the budget and manage the day to day operations;
- You are 100% responsible for your successes and your failures;
- You determine how you spend your time and how the time spent on different things, ultimately supports your life's vision and happiness;
- You embrace the strategic planning necessary to achieve your goals;
- You make the investments necessary to grow, thrive and succeed.

If you are saying to yourself, "Wow, I have never thought about my life in that way," you are not alone. Most people, perhaps women in particular, do not think of themselves as the CEO of their life. It is time to change that. To shift your mindset and start acting like the CEO of your life, begin by asking yourself the following questions:

1. *What is the purpose of my life? Do I have a Vision, Mission & Values Statement?*

One of the first things you have learned, if you have ever started a business, thought about starting a business or taken a business course, is that having clear vision, mission and values statements is critical to the success of a business. So, if you think clearly articulated vision, mission and values are critical for the success of a business, hopefully you can see that they also contribute to success in your life. It is particularly important that women, especially working moms, have a vision and goals for their personal life because, as women, we too often focus only on what we can do for others. Rarely do we assess our own needs and acknowledge how having our own lives in order positions us to do all the things we want to do for others (family, community, workplace, etc.). Articulating a vision and goals keeps us focused on what is really important. It helps us produce strategies for attaining the results we want to see in our lives.

If you do not have a clear vision, mission and values statement, draft one today. If you do not know where to start, there is help on the internet. Or, you might consider working with someone who can help you develop one. Remember, "If you don't know where you're going, any road will take you there."

Your personal vision statement should be written in first person and must contains statements that list of the goal you want. For example, your personal vision statement could be "I am a high-achieving working mom who excels in business, is committed to working in the community and has plenty of time to spend quality time with the ones I love and to practice self-care."

Your personal mission statement guides you. It helps you clearly articulate what success looks like for you; it should be action-oriented. For example, your mission statement might be "To live a life full of happiness, purpose and success. To have a strong marriage based on love, mutual respect and friendship. To raise happy and healthy children who know how much their mom loves them and who grow up to be successful happy adults who look back on their childhood as a happy time. To have a successful and fulfilling career that, is not only financially beneficial, but affects the lives of others in a positive way."

A personal values statement is a short description of the values that are most important to you. This is critical; it is easy to become involved in things that have no value and that can pull you off course from the things that *are* really important. Having a personal values statement will help you stay true to what is important and will also help you align yourself with things professionally that will make you happy. For example, if you are working for a company that does not share your values, you will be miserable. Another benefit to having and living by your personal values statement is that when you are operate in your core values (honesty, integrity, compassion, etc.), it draws to you others with those same values. Thus, the personal values statement positions you to do business with, associate with and become friends with people who share your values. An example of your values statement might be, "I operate in integrity and honesty. I will show compassion to those with whom I come into contact. I will not procrastinate. I will always do my best work."

2. *What are the goals of my life?*

Having vision, mission and values statements is a critical beginning point. However, once you have identified where you want to go, you must identify S.M.A.R.T (specific, measurable, attainable, relevant and timely) goals to help you get there. Goals should be personal – including goals for your family – as well as professional. Any good CEO engages in ongoing goal setting and evaluation and makes adjustments necessary to ensure that the goals are attained. As the CEO of my life, I am constantly setting, monitoring and evaluating the achievement of my goals.

A good tool for goal setting is to create your own vision board. A vision board is the visual depiction of the things you want to see in your life and a great way to help you manifest your goals. In addition to creating my own personal vision board, my family annually works on a family vision board. We schedule a fun family night activity where we might order pizza and work together on family goals for the year. This vision board includes what we want to do as a family (e.g., family night activities, family vacations, etc.) and helps us maintain family time as an important priority. Because the mind responds strongly to visual stimulation, representing goals with pictures and images on a vision board strengthens and stimulates the emotions. Emotions, in turn, activate the Law of Attraction, which says that focusing on positive (or negative) things brings those things into your life. In other words, when you create a mental image of what you want to achieve, you draw into your life what you visualize.

3. *Who comprises the board of directors in my life?*

In corporate America, the major responsibilities of a Board of Directors are to assess the overall strategy and direction of the corporation and to protect corporate assets. Boards of Directors often advise the CEO when major decisions need to made.

Boards of Directors are invaluable to the long-term strategic positioning of a company; they are equally invaluable to strategically pursuing the goals of your life.

Many of us have a small group of people to whom we reach out whenever we make a major decision. The group typically includes family members, friends, relatives, etc. These individuals no doubt care deeply about you and have your best interests at heart. However, their concern for you does not automatically equip them to strategically help you reach your goals. Frankly, some people do not have the capacity to help you reach your goals because of their own limiting beliefs. If you really want to achieve the success you desire and deserve, consider forming a *personal* **Board of Directors**, putting just as much thought into selecting personal board members as you would into selecting corporate board members. For example, consider selecting personal board members whose specific strengths, experiences and skills can contribute to pursuit of your life ambitions and goals. Consider, also, tapping into wisdom that you might have overlooked. As a working mother, I routinely tap into the expertise of other working moms (e.g., my own mother) who have successfully built great careers and raised accomplished children. A carefully chosen personal Board of Directors can not only provide you with wisdom and support, but can strategically accelerate progress towards your goals.

4. Do I have a strategic plan?

Setting goals for your life is essential, but not sufficient. A good CEO knows that a strategic plan is necessary for successfully mapping the road to goal attainment. As the CEO of your life, you must develop a strategic plan that establishes your priorities and helps you focus energy on the actions needed to achieve the outcomes you have laid out. Given your busy schedules and your many roles and responsibilities, a strategic plan is particularly important as you work towards work-life integration. Merely desiring work-life integration is not enough – you must articulate a plan and strategies for achieving it.

A **personal strategic plan** is a <u>must-have</u> tool. A thoughtfully constructed strategic plan will help you: (a) determine where you are, (b) identify what's important, (c) assess your

current strengths and opportunities, (d) identify how you will measure your success and (e) put in place strategies to hold yourself accountable. Such a plan can help take you to places you never thought possible. If you haven't already done so, take the time to lay out a strategic plan now. If uninterrupted time with family is a priority, determine how you will make that happen. If taking time off from work to chaperone a child's field trip or taking a vacation during the summer is a goal, map out the steps to achieve those outcomes. Having a strategic plan will help keep you on track and focused on the future.

5. *What are my daily functions and how do they align with my purpose?*

In the work environment, you know what you need to do every day to accomplish your work. When you arrive at the office, you know you need to check emails, return phone calls, attend scheduled meetings, etc. However, you likely do not conceptualize your "off work" time as having the same specificity of to-dos.

As you review your goals and strategic plan, think about the daily activities you must perform to fulfill them. For example, if learning something new is one of your goals, sign up for a class, buy a book or look for someone to teach you. If supporting your child's desire to play a team sport is one of your goals, determine what you need to do so that s/he can attend practice and games. Each day, the items on your to-do list should align with your priorities and move you toward your goals. If the things that are currently part of your daily activities do not move you in the right direction, consider eliminating them from your daily routine.

6. *Who are the stakeholders in my life? Who are the people most invested in my success?*

Knowing who your stakeholders are keeps you focused on why work-life integration is important and pushes you to prioritize how you spend your time. The stakeholders in your life are the people for whom you do what you do – most likely your spouse, your parents, your children, etc. These are people who love and support you. They are also individuals who, if *you* are happy, fulfilled and successful, are also likely to be happy, fulfilled, and successful. Corporate CEOs answer to their stakeholders (i.e., shareholders), who expect a return on their investment – a ROI. Although your stakeholders may not expect a ROI, you should feel obligated to give them one. Your intuitive desire to make them proud, the quality time you spend with them, the meaningful example your life provides them – any of these can constitute a ROI for your stakeholders.

Conclusion

Ever since I shifted my mindset and began seeing myself as and acting as the CEO of my life, I have been able to take charge of what happens in my life and able to truly focus on what is important. A CEO knows that she must take responsibility for what happens in her company. She cannot pass the buck and blame others when things don't go as they should. Rather, she addresses issues head-on and finds a way to right the ship when things go wrong. That is how I have approached my life. I know people who become discouraged when unpleasant things happen in their lives; they tend to wallow in their misfortune or blame other people. They take no responsibility for making things better and so they do not move forward.

I have come to realize that, as the CEO of my life, I am 100% responsible for my successes, my failures, my happiness and my time. Do not misunderstand me; I am not saying that I am all-powerful – I know that God is in control. But in knowing that God is in control, I also know that He would never give me anything that I cannot handle. I know that He wants me to live a happy, fulfilled life and that He has fully equipped me with the tools to live that life. With that understanding, I know that I can impact my life. I choose to be happy; if things I do not want occur in my life, I don't become depressed. Instead, I look for a way to change things or, in the event that I cannot change them, I look for a way to change my reaction to them.

Homework

Put what we have discussed into action.

1. Write a vision statement for your life.
2. Write a mission statement for your life.
3. Write a Values statement for your life.
4. What are some of your life's goals?

5. Write down the people who you want to be your Board of Directors.

6. Draft a personal strategic plan

7. Who are your stakeholders and what is the "return on investment" you desire to give them?

RULE # 2

<><><><><><><><><><><><><><><><><><>

Identify and Monitor the Big "Why?" of Your Life

O ften we are consumed by *how* to do something (how to have a better life, how make more money, how to spend time with family, etc.). In our fixation on *how*, we overlook *why* we want to do these things. Yet, if we don't know the *why*, the *how* makes little difference. Your big *why* is something or someone about which you are passionate. Your *why* emotionally charges you. It motivates and pushes you to keep going even when you feel like giving up. It is your life's purpose. Although not something from which you gain instant gratification, your why will continue to drive you and may change during the course of your life. For example, your why as a single person, just starting your career, may change when you become a working mom, juggling multiple businesses. It may change again as you approach the brink of retirement. The one thing about your big *why* that, hopefully does not change, is that it gives you a sense of something bigger than yourself.

Regularly Revisit Your Big Why

Once you have identified your big *why*, periodic reflection about the why is important. First, reflection will help you assess the need to change or rearticulate your why. Additionally, reflection is essential in order to determine whether your behavior is in alignment with your big why. For example, we work to make money and to have the finer things in life, so that we can achieve happiness. However, if we work so much that we are stressed and not able to spend time with the ones we love, then we are not happy.

Two occurrences from my life were particularly valuable in emphasizing how periodic reflection on the big *why* helps to maintain focus on what is <u>most</u> important in our life and also supports consistency between what we say or think and what we actually do.

Example One

Many years ago, I took a business development class in which the instructor discussed how to deal with difficult or non-paying clients. He asked how many people had in their office pictures of people and places they loved. Virtually everyone raised a hand. The instructor then asked how many of us had clients who paid slowly or not at all. Again, almost everyone raised a hand. The instructor asked how many of us would choose to spend time with our family or in places we loved, rather than with non-paying or slow paying clients. Again, most hands went up. The instructor then made two simple, yet profound, suggestions. First, he suggested that we turn all of the beloved pictures in our office so that they faced us. Second, he suggested that the next time we were on the phone with or sitting across the desk from a non-paying/ slow paying client, we remind ourselves that we could be with the ones we love, rather than working for free. His suggestions created a real "aha!" moment for me. At that time, I was doing a lot of pro bono work. Because my heart is so big, I always wanted to help people in need. However, that class helped me realize that I could allow my heart to help people and not go broke or be away from the ones I love to do it.

After that class, I completely changed my fee structure and how I require clients to pay. I built into my overall business plan the number of clients I could afford to take on a pro-bono basis. I still give back to those in need, but when I meet my quota, I politely decline any more clients who cannot pay my fee. This shift gave me the opportunity to work less and make more, thus, giving me time and finances to spend on my family.

Example Two
I have a full-time job and, though I work for myself, my schedule can fill up very quickly, sometimes

requiring me to work for eight to ten hours a day. Consequently, my children go to an aftercare school program when the traditional school day has ended and I pick them up close to 6 p.m. One day when I was picking up my middle child from elementary school, she asked me why she couldn't be a "car rider" and then go to the park with me after school, like many of her friends. I realized that the kids to whom my daughter was referring had stay-at-home moms who picked their kids up at 2:30 and then had play dates with them in the park. I explained to my daughter that *her* mommy did not have a schedule that would allow her to do that every day. Although she seemed to accept and understand my answer, she looked very disappointed. The next week when I was planning my schedule, I made it a point not to schedule anything on Friday after 2 p.m. so that I could surprise my daughter by picking her up from school and taking her to the park for a picnic. I arrived at school on that Friday and had the staff call for her and tell her that she was not to go to aftercare because she was a "car rider." At 2:30, I was standing in the line with the stay-at-home moms, waiting to take my princess to the park. When she came out and saw me, she came running over and gave me a big hug, as always. Then she asked if she had a doctor's appointment. I told her, "No," that mommy wanted to take her to the park to play. The look on her face was priceless! In addition, I invited my mother to join us. She scheduled a late lunch so she could join us and we made a girls afternoon of it.

Align Your *Why* with Your Actions and be Sure to Include *You*

I've always known that my family is the reason I do what I do. I work hard to help put food on the table, to keep a roof over their heads, to provide a quality of life that allows them a broad range of experiences and opportunities. However, it wasn't until that moment described above that I realized that the *why* I was working so hard, was also the *why* I needed *not* to work so hard. At that moment, my true *why* became more apparent to me! Work-life integration stopped being an aspirational cliché and became a lifestyle I committed to implementing.

As I contemplated this commitment, I acknowledged that I had chosen to be an entrepreneur so that I might have flexibility, independence and autonomy in my work life. I acknowledged that I had accepted the need to work as hard as I could to build successful businesses so that I might provide well for my family – my why. Yet, I was also compelled to acknowledge that, while I was working hard in my businesses, I was missing moments in the lives of my family that business titles and finances can neither replace nor restore. I know that I am not alone in acknowledging this truth; it is why many women put their professional dreams on hold when they have a family. They feel torn between investment in their career and fulfillment of their responsibilities at home. However, what has become apparent to me – as I hope it will to you – is that my why can and must address my personal aspirations, as well as the welfare and needs of those who are most important to me. Consequently, my why has become more inclusive – it now includes me.

As mothers, we teach our kids that they can do anything to which they set their minds. We teach them to work hard and to never give up. But what message do we send when our mouths tell them one thing and they see us doing something different? When children and family are your big why, they are also the reason you must be true to yourself and neither minimize nor suppress your gifts, your talents, your dreams or your goals.

Homework

Once you figure out your BIG WHY, gather tangible representations of your why (i.e., pictures, audio recordings, etc.). Place the items on your desk or use them as the screensaver on your phone and computer. In other words, keep these representations front and center so you are constantly reminded why you work so hard AND why you should *not* work so hard.

RULE # 3

*Organize the Content
of Your Life*

A key strategy for achieving work-life integration is to set priorities. As high achieving women, we are constantly pulled in multiple directions at the same time – juggling multiple responsibilities, including work deadlines and children's obligations; managing relationships with our spouse and significant others; and taking care of ourselves. We want to be everything to everyone, so it is sometimes hard to focus on what is most important. Given limited time and resources, we must prioritize to make sure those things that are most important are being accomplished. In this section, I will detail further, strategies I have used that helped me move closer to my goal of work-life integration.

Establish and Manage Priorities

With all the hats I wear and all the things competing for my time, it is easy to become overwhelmed.

Sometimes I walk into my law office or my home office, look at the things on my desk and don't know where to begin. A cluttered desk is a sign of a cluttered and confused mind and a confused mind does not accomplish anything. The best way to declutter your mind and start the day or week off right is to set priorities. The following are the steps that I have found helpful in prioritizing and managing multiple work, personal and family commitments, responsibilities and demands.

Steps for Managing Priorities

1. Identify your long-term goals and objectives
2. Identify priorities that align with your goals
3. List your priorities on a TO DO list.
   a. Identify the 5 most important tasks for each subsequent day. (Do this the night before, so you can hit the ground running in the morning.) Consider your most pressing work, family and personal time commitments.
   b. ALWAYS include leisure time for yourself and quality time with family and friends.
4. Determine the importance of the priority items on your list by asking yourself the following questions:
   a. Why am I doing this?
   b. How does this task align with my goals and objectives?

    c. Is this an urgent task?

    d. Can someone else do this task?

5. Determine the ranking of the priorities on your "to do" list by dividing tasks on the list into the following three categories:

    a. Must Do Items

    These essential items often include crucial deadlines, time sensitive matters, opportunities for success or promotion, management directives or customer requests.

    b. Should Do Items

    These are items of value but do not include significant deadlines. These items are important but can be postponed temporarily, if necessary.

    c. Nice to Do Items

    These items could be eliminated or postponed until later.

6. Review your priority list weekly, rearranging items as necessary to reflect the changing demands on your time.

7. Stay focused on your priorities:

    a. Don't over commit; limit your priorities to 2-3 per day

    If you list too many it is easy to spread yourself too thin and not really accomplish anything.

b. Stay laser focused on completing these 2-3 priorities before moving on to the next ones.

While establishment and management of the priorities of your life are critical to achieving work-life integration, several other steps are also essential. The remainder of this section addresses three additional strategies/approaches that support successful pursuit of work-life integration. Specifically, these strategies include: (a) creating and celebrating milestones and benchmarks, (b) identifying and utilizing accountability partners, and (c) knowing and respecting your limits.

Create and Celebrate Milestones and Benchmarks

The goal you have set to achieve work-life integration will not be quickly, nor easily achieved; persistence, patience and much unlearning and rewiring may be necessary to change habitual ways of believing, thinking and acting. In order to establish and maintain an optimistic and energetic focus on your goals, objectives and priorities: identify some milestones or benchmarks leading to the desired outcome; track your progress; and then celebrate your attainment of these milestones/benchmarks.

For example, a few years ago, my husband and I took a financial ministry course. It taught us, among other things, how to get out of debt and create savings centered on our life's goals. As we created our plan for saving and paying off debt, the instructor encouraged us to set smaller goals and to celebrate once they were accomplished. For instance, one of our goals was to save seven to 10 months of expenses as emergency savings. Rather than delaying a celebration until that ultimate goal was reached, we set interim milestones and benchmarks along the path to that goal. Thus, whenever we had saved one month of expenses, we would celebrate by going out to dinner. Not an expensive dinner because of course that would be counter-productive to the goal of saving but a nice dinner that we paid for in cash. These benchmark rewards represented small "wins:" They gave us an opportunity to see our progress and they motivated us to continue pursuing our goal. It also gave us some quality family time together.

Identify and Utilize Accountability Partners

One of the best strategies for maintaining focus on your goals, objectives and priorities is to find and utilize an "accountability partner." An accountability partner is a trusted confidant who becomes part of your support team and holds you accountable to reach your goals. Your accountability partner can be a family member, a friend or co-worker. S/he will be your cheerleader, but should also be available to hold you to your commitments when you waver. In other words, an effective accountability partner plays a dual role: a cheerleader who lauds your efforts and a coach who pushes you toward your limits. This individual should be supportive and encouraging. Yet, s/he should assertive enough to give you positive, as well as negative feedback, and should be comfortable doing so. You must choose your AP with care. For example, you would not want to choose someone whose appropriate performance in the dual role of an AP would negatively impact a familial relationship.

Know and Respect Your Limits

Given the many hats I wear, I receive requests to do many, many things: *Can you come and give a welcome? Can you come speak to my girl scout troop? Can you come do this? Can you come do that?* If I said, "Yes" to every invitation I get, I would be on the run 24/7 and would always be away from my family. Nevertheless, as a public official, I have tried to do as many things as possible. On a couple of occasions, I had scheduled myself so tightly that I didn't even build in travel time. Consequently, I showed up late to an event and when that event ran overtime, I was late to event number two and number three, etc., thus creating an entire day of running late. One day, I found myself in the car, literally all day long, going to different events. Because I was late picking up kids, I had no family time in the evening. That kind of schedule made me miserable and did not work for anyone: I inevitably let someone down because I couldn't maintain it. I was forced to realize that, in doing things that were important to other people, I was letting down the people who depend on me the most.

At any rate, I have learned that you have to know your limits. Additionally, you have to create reasonable expectations around those limits so that you don't disappoint yourself, you don't disappoint other people and you don't overwhelm yourself. Each day is different; each day your stamina, your interests, your energy, or your schedule may differ. Because every day is different, there is no magic formula for getting things done. However, one thing that is consistent is your need to know your limits – what you can and cannot accomplish in a day – what you are and are not comfortable with doing. Overcommitment, knowing that you do not have enough time to fulfill that commitment or that you will forfeit sleep or effectiveness, can lead to stress and feelings of being overwhelmed. You mig overcommit regardless, so as not to let someone down. Then, when you cannot meet the commitment . . . Surprise! You have still let that person down and you have let yourself down, as well. Despite the tendency of many women to think that we are superwomen, we cannot do everything. We must be honest with ourselves, acknowledge our limitations and create reasonable expectations regarding what we can and cannot do at a given time; everyone will be better for it.

When I was in high school I was diagnosed with a neurological disease called *myasthenia gravis*. I rarely mention it publicly, but since I am in the public eye, most people have noticed physical signs of the disease. I know that my myasthenia is aggravated by stress and, even more, by being tired. If I am not getting sufficient sleep, if I'm running from place to place, one of my eyelids begins to droop making one eye appear smaller than the other. Knowing that this is a result of being over tired and knowing the demands of my schedule, I have learned to adjust my activities accordingly. For example, during campaign season when the need to make public appearances increases, I make special efforts to accommodate my body's needs and avoid becoming overtired. For example: (a) I politely decline requests that over commit me: "I'm sorry, I cannot handle that request;" (b) I become negotiator-in-chief: "Mom's sorry, she can't do that right now; Let's look at my calendar and you can help me choose a date when we can do that;" and (c) I make sure to schedule additional opportunities for rest – the 20 minute "power nap" has become my friend!

Homework

This week, use the *Must Do, Have To Do and Nice To Do Method* to prioritize your To Do List. Use the following template:

TO DO LIST

Date: /   /

A: MUST DO

_____

_____

_____

_____

B: SHOULD DO

_____

_____

_____

_____

C: NICE TO DO

_____

_____

_____

_____

RULE # 4

◇◇◇◇◇◇◇◇◇◇◇◇◇◇◇◇◇◇◇◇◇◇◇◇

Create Memories

*H*aving a great job, making a lot of money and holding prestigious positions are meaningful and enjoyable outcomes of your hard work. However, if those outcomes come at the expense of spending quality time with the ones you love, you are not really successful. Any relationships that are important to you must be nurtured and the best way to nurture those relationships is with your quality time. I know of several relationships that have been destroyed because one partner was too busy to show the other that s/he was important. Carving time out of your hectic schedule to create memories and just enjoy small things can strengthen your marriage/ relationship and foster a priceless bond with your children – who won't be young forever.

Invest in Experiences

An article I once read stated that adults surveyed remembered the time they spent with loved ones more than the fancy trips they took. Similarly, a San Francisco State University study found that people who spent money on experiences, rather than on material items, were happier and felt the money was better spent. The thrill of purchasing things fades quickly, but the joy and memories of experiences, can last a lifetime.

Last summer, we took our daughter to camp in North Carolina. As we were riding up I-95 towards the South Carolina-North Carolina state line, I started seeing signs for South of the Border. Seeing the signs brought back memories of my childhood. Every year when we traveled "up north," my dad would always want to stop at South of the Border to get some ice cream. Since we were had plenty of time until we had to check her in at Camp, we decided to stop at South of the Border and have my girls experience the same things that I did as I grew up. It was funny at first because my children did not quite understand what the draw was for South of the Border. There were no rides. No big amusement parks. No water slides. Just Pedro and his big hat, an ice cream store and lots of gift items.

As we stopped at South of the Border and got our ice cream, I shared with them about "going up north" when I was as a child - how we would stop at South of the Border - and the memories I had of our family just hanging out there having a really good time. Although there were no amusement park there, my children ended up having a pretty good time. So much so, that at the end of the week, when we picked up my little one from Camp, as we came back through the same North Carolina–South Carolina state line, my children wanted to stop again at South of the Border for ice cream.

The moral of the story is ... you never know what experiences your children will enjoy. So, think about the things that you enjoyed when you were younger and expose your children to those same types of experiences. They may not include video games or water parks or other fancy things that we have nowadays, but they will provide your kids an opportunity to build lifelong memories that they may, one day, be able to share with their own children.

Enjoy the Little Things

When we think about the things that make us happy, we tend to think about big things. Focusing on major milestones and achievements does indeed bring joy; but the joy is temporary. Lasting fulfillment, on the other hand, comes from enjoying small everyday moments. Memories we create during everyday moments – date night, family night – are those we are most likely to appreciate when are kids are grown, when we retire, when loved ones are gone.

Although we tend to think of life as the passage of days, weeks, years and decades, life is made up of moments. Making deliberate plans to enjoy little things during all the moments of your life is the best way to ensure that you do not wake up one day full of regrets. But, make no mistake – planning *is* required if you want the *enjoyment* pan of your life's scale to outweigh the *regrets* pan. Consider the weight currently in each pan by reflecting on a typical day and asking yourself what moments stand out for you:

1. the stress of trying to do it all?
2. the things that didn't get done?
3. the disappointment in yourself because of what you forgot to do?
4. the disappointment in yourself because of what you failed to accomplish?
5. a gloomy feeling about how far you are from the top of your profession/business/career?

If your assessment indicates that it is time for you to change your enjoyment vs. regret ratio, the following suggestions may be helpful.

SUGGESTIONS FOR INCREASING THE ENJOYMENT IN YOUR LIFE:
It's the Little Things that Count

---

1. Pay attention, each day, to at least one or two moments that worked out well for you. Don't beat yourself up and focus on things that

didn't go as planned. Instead, pay attention and celebrate the things you were able to accomplish. For example, if you have 10 items on your "To-Do" list and accomplish 3, celebrate that you at least completed the 3 tasks and make a plan on how to tackle the remaining 7 on the next day.

2. Take advantage of ongoing or unusual events to create memories with the ones you love. August 10 each year is National Smores Day. Here, in South Carolina, that is almost always one of the hottest days of the year. Most people would think it crazy to build a campfire in the backyard. Nevertheless, that is exactly what we did! Last year, we had a particularly busy summer. My oldest went away to 3 different week long camps and my husband and I both had several work related conferences, so we were travelling non-stop all summer. My babies love S'mores. Roasting marshmallows and watching the heat from them melt the chocolate is probably more fun than eating the fireside treats. So when we had an evening (August 10) and we were all home together, we decided to pull out the fire pit and make some S'mores. They were delicious. But the best part of our National S'mores Day was the quality family time we spend together, enjoying our backyard and each other's company.

3. Reconsider your perception of "affordability" as it relates to creating memories.

   We have all struggled with being able to "afford" fun time away from work. As an entrepreneur, I used to find it hard to get away from the office. Work took priority, even though I didn't mean it to. I would not plan any lengthy get away with the family because I didn't think I could afford to take the time. I told myself, "If I am not working, I am not getting paid and I need to get paid so my family can eat." As my kids get older, I have come to appreciate that not only *can* I afford to make the time, I can't afford *not* to. And, creating memories need not cost a lot of money. Consider the following fun, cost-effective activities that will surely make your children happy.

INEXPENSIVE ACTIVITIES FOR CREATING MEMORIES

---

1. *Play Day.*

   Take a day to do nothing but play. Ride your bikes, do a scavenger hunt around the house, play a game of tag or hopscotch out in the yard or go to the nearest park. You can also pack a picnic lunch, allowing everyone to help fix the items for lunch.

2. *Craft Day*

   Pull out the crayons, construction paper and glitter and spend the day being creative.

   Tap into your creative side and let it run wild. During our creative days, I like to create vision boards for the whole family (even if you have already done one) or a visual bucket list. You can also check the internet for easy-to-do at home craft ideas.

3. *Movie Day*

   Spend the day watching movies together. Allow everyone to pick their favorite movie and take turns watching that person's choice together. You can even stay in your pajamas and treat it like one big family pajama party. Pop some popcorn, relax and have fun.

4. *Nature Day*

   Go for a nature walk or a hike. If you have a state park near you, that is a great place to go and explore. You can also go camping in the backyard. Set up tents and pull out the sleeping bags and flashlights. This is a great adventure, without even leaving your home.

5. *Reading Day*

   Go to the library and spend the day exploring the world through books. You can find books of interest for the whole family. The public library also has story time and other activities that the kids will love.

6. *Culinary Day*

   Plan a day for exploring culinary arts. Kids love to cook. And not only will you be teaching your kids a critical life skill, but the activity can also reinforce math, science and artistic concepts. Children can take turns choosing the focus of each culinary day. For example, one day might focus on a meal course (e.g., entree or dessert or appetizer). Or, a day might focus on a particular food type (e.g., bread, pizza). Or you can even jazz it up a bit and create a theme for the day. Italian and Mexican days are our favorite. In addition to preparing the food, you will spend quality time together eating what you prepared

No matter what you choose to do, remember that it's not where you go or how much money you spend. It is about the time that you spend together. The memories you are creating for your family are **priceless**.

Homework

Make a list of 10 things you can do with the ones you love. However, nothing can cost over $50. (Hint: Start by considering the things you enjoyed when you were little)

RULE # 5

~~~~~~~~~~~~~~~~~~~~~~~~~~~~~~

Create a Bucket List

*I*n Chapter 4, when we discussed creating memories, I briefly mentioned creating a bucket list. A bucket list is a list of experiences or achievements that a person hopes to have or accomplish during their lifetime. It can include places, financial goals you'd like to achieve, experiences you want to share with loved ones, things you want to expose your kids to and random fun things you wish to do – like karaoke. Having a bucket list encourages you to set goals outside of work. It makes you think about how you want to experience life. Life is short; if you are always wishing to do something, but never actually planning to do it, you will wake up one day with a lot of regrets.

I have always wanted to go on a Disney Cruise. For years I heard people say how amazing the cruise is and how much fun it is for adults, as well as the children. But, every year something came up: either I didn't have the money or I didn't have the time, etc. As the years passed, I kept telling myself, "Maybe next year." As *next year* became the next, I began to realize that I was allowing myself to put off things because I didn't make them a priority. So,

I created a bucket list for 2017 and the first item on it was a Disney Cruise! Looking at all of the items on my priority list, I knew that the only way I would implement the Disney Cruise item was to actually schedule it. I looked at my calendar, picked dates that I knew I could travel, called a travel agent, booked the trip and set up a payment plan, so cost would not be an issue. My *some*day became a *specific* day.

Creating a bucket list is a productivity strategy that can move you one step closer to work-life integration. As you start putting things into your life that bring you great joy, you naturally become more focused at work because you have a compelling personal life that makes you want to leave the office on time. Writing a book was on my bucket list. My first book was published on 2015; this is my second book.

Our family has a bucket list exclusively related to travel. It includes all the places we want go, such as Nickelodeon resort in Punta Cana and Atlantis in the Bahamas. Taking my children to a Broadway play, going to the Disney resort in Hawaii, attending the Kids Choice Awards, travelling to South Africa and visiting every state in the country are also on our bucket list. As a fun way to help us visualize the goal of visiting every state, I printed a coloring page map of the United States. Then one day, as a family activity, we each colored every state that we have visited. Now, every time we visit a new state, we come home and color that state. The visual representation of the places we visit gives the kids something fun to do as we work toward our goal. Our intent is to have the entire map colored by the time the kids graduate from high school.

Approach the items on your bucket list just as you would a "to do" list. Creating a bucket list makes your desires more tangible and can provide an opportunity for the family to discuss its collective desires. Checking off the items on your bucket list will give you (and your family) a sense of accomplishment. To summarize, creating a bucket list can: (a) remind you of your big why, (b) help you enjoy the small things and (c) push you to make time to create memories, as discussed in the previous chapters.

Homework

Start Your Bucket List. Encourage every member of the family to add something to the list.

RULE # 6

<><><><><><><><><><><><><><><><><><><>

Deal with Mom Guilt

When my oldest daughter was young, I was learning to juggle being a full-time attorney and a councilwoman, while getting used to my role as mom. One day when my daughter was about three years-old, I had worked all day at the law firm and had to attend a community meeting that evening. My husband was out of town, so I had to take my daughter with me. I picked her up from school and, since we were not going directly home, I went through the convenient McDonalds Drive Thru. I ordered a kids' *Happy Meal* - chicken fingers, milk and apple slices. Although I knew this wasn't the best meal my daughter could have had, I didn't think it was the end of the world.

When I got to the meeting, I set my daughter up at a table with her Happy Meal and a coloring book and proceeded to take my seat at the front of the room. As I got to my seat, one of the neighborhood leaders looked over at me and said, "You are feeding your child McDonalds? That is not a real dinner." I was, of course, taken aback by the judgment I received at that moment. I thought I was doing a good thing by honoring the request to be present at this meeting while juggling my priority to my family. It was not as though I'd stuck my child in a corner with a bag of Skittles! This was my first face-to-face experience of *Mom shaming.*

The woman who called me out was older and had probably raised her children at a time when mom or grandma was there to make a home-cooked meal for the family every night. So, I recognize that her frame of reference was probably very different than mine; nevertheless that comment stung. I went home questioning whether I was making choices for me at the expense of my family. I began wondering if the Supermom *S* I had imagined was on my chest was a misrepresentation and whether what I thought I was doing successfully was really a failure.

All moms experience *mom guilt* from time to time, whether we work outside the home or work in the home. We feel guilty about the choices we must make to keep moving forward in our career. We feel guilty enjoying some adult time. We experience guilt leaving our child for the first time to go back to work after maternity leave. We feel guilty about not being able to breastfeed or about not being able to chaperone the class field trip. We all have times when we feel inadequate as a parent. We feel that everyone else is doing it better or that we don't measure up to others. We put pressure on ourselves to be perfect. When we begin to venture on a guilt trip, it is essential that we remind ourselves of two inarguable realities: (a) no one is perfect and (b) parenting is not a competitive sport! There are always things that you could be doing better and there are always other parents doing something you wish you could do. I talked in a previous chapter about my daughter wanting to go to the park after school like some of the other children. As a full time, working mom, I did not have the luxury of picking her up every day at 2:30 and then taking her to the park to play before going home. While I am happy for the moms who could do that, my not being able to do so didn't diminish my *goodness* as a mother; I had nothing to feel guilty about.

In a time where social media and reality TV shape our frame of reference, it is easy to look at someone else's life (or the life they want you to see) and compare what you feel is not going right in yours. But remember that no one can be a better mom to your children than you. Are there some things you could do differently? Of course there are. But you must make choices to address *your* own needs and lifestyle, rather than to gain the approval of others. If your children are healthy and happy, that is what matters most. At the end of the day, no one is perfect – and you can stop believing people who try to tell you they are.

My best friend has shirt that reads, "perfectly imperfect." I love that shirt! That shirt acknowledges that we are not perfect and grants us permission to be imperfect. We do not need to beat ourselves up about not being perfect; God loves us anyway. He shows us grace and mercy everyday. Grace is the undeserved favor that we receive from God, no questions asked. So what if you forgot to pick up the dry cleaning? So what if you buy a cake from the grocery store? So what if you have dirty dishes in the sink? These things do not signal the end of the world. Let's all stop being so hard on ourselves and allow ourselves the opportunity to be imperfect. Let's remember that Mary Poppins only exists at Disney!

Homework

We all need grace, but showing ourselves grace is one of the hardest things to do. You can work toward the ability to show yourself grace by showing grace to others. Find opportunities to show grace to another woman. Contact a friend you haven't talked to in a while or a mom from the PTO. Be a good listener; it is likely that your conversation will reveal a challenge she is having. Give her a pep talk; let her know that she has the ability to meet whatever challenge she is facing. Showing grace to those around you may make it easier to show yourself grace.

RULE # 7

Express Gratitude:
Count Your Blessings,
Not Your Problems

When I decided to become certified as a personal and executive coach, I chose Valorie Burton's program, CaPP. I had always loved Valorie and her spirit, but once I started her program and understood that it was based on positive psychology, my choice was validated – I knew I had selected the right program. One of the things that experts in the field of positive psychology teach is that the mental state of being thankful benefits the giver of thanks as much as the receiver.

For many years, every night, before I go to bed, I make a list of things for which I am grateful. Some of those things are: my family, true friendships, life experiences and life's setbacks, because they have taught me valuable lessons. The challenge I give myself is that I cannot mention the same thing more than once in a month. Consequently, after I get past the obvious things (e.g., family, health, job, etc.), I must dig deep to identify something for which to be grateful. It is an awesome experience; even when things are not going great, I must come up with something. This exercise helps me keep my life in perspective and truly keeps me focused on my blessings.

Gratitude can have a profound effect on our health and happiness. Research shows that an attitude of gratitude increases self-worth and self-esteem, combats negative emotions such as stress and anger and releases endorphins in the brain that produce a sense of well-being. Two psychologists, Michael McCollough of Southern Methodist University in Dallas, Texas, and Robert Emmons of the University of California at Davis, wrote an article about an experiment they conducted on gratitude and its impact on well-being. The study split several hundred people into three different groups. All participants were asked to keep daily diaries. The first group was directed to keep a diary of the events that occurred during the day. No direction was given regarding whether to chronicle good or bad things. The second group was directed to record their unpleasant experiences. The third group was instructed to make a daily list of things for which they were grateful. McCollough and Emmons found that group three – the "gratitude group" – reported higher levels of alertness, enthusiasm, determination, optimism, and energy. In addition, individuals in the gratitude group experienced less depression and stress, were more likely to help others, exercised more regularly, and made greater progress toward achieving personal goals.

Other behavioral and psychological research studies, as well, have shown that surprising life improvements can stem from the practice of gratitude. Expressing gratitude does not mean your life is perfect; it just means you are aware of your blessings. Gratitude shifts your focus from what your life lacks, to the abundance that is already present. Giving thanks makes people happier and more resilient. It strengthens relationships, improves health and reduces stress. Thus, gratitude, as confirmed by empirical evidence, is an essential ingredient of a happy, fulfilling life.

If you can learn to express gratitude for little things that are already present in your day, if you can focus on the small, yet meaningful, moments in your life, your relationship to happiness will begin to transform in the most beautiful of ways. However, you must *practice*: you must make giving thanks a priority – part of your daily routine. Consider dedicating five minutes every morning and evening to write about those things for which you are most grateful. Do not repeat the same thing for two weeks. The more often you write in your gratitude journal, the more you will begin to notice little things that fill your heart with appreciation. When you have practiced gratitude on a committed and regular basis, you should notice an increase in your sense of contentment and equilibrium: small things that used to overwhelm you may seem insignificant; disappointments may seem less disappointing; your ability to focus on what really matters may seem truer.

Following are some of the simple ways by which you can express your gratitude:

- Say "thank you"

    Saying "thank you" requires little effort, yet many of us take this simple task for granted. In the hurry and bustle through our lives, too many of us forget to thank others for simple courtesies: the assistance we receive from the bagger in a grocery store, the service we receive from the waiter in a restaurant. Hearing "thank you" makes the service provider feel noticed and valued. Saying "thank you" whenever someone performs a service for us – whether large or small – provides an opportunity to express gratitude, thereby positively impacting our own health and happiness.

- Send thank you cards

    Even more rare than saying "thank you," is the art of sending a thank you note. When I was growing up, my mother insisted that I hand write thank you notes for every Christmas gift, birthday gift and graduation recognition. These days, it is increasingly uncommon to receive a thank you note of any kind, much less a handwritten one. Think about individuals who do special things for you whose service you could acknowledge by sending a handwritten note of thanks. It might be the sales associate who helped you find that special dress or the secretary at your child's school. I promise you that note will brighten your day, as well as theirs.

- Buy an inexpensive gift as a token of appreciation

  One way to maximize your gift-giving tokens of appreciation is to purchase inexpensive items during trips or vacations you take. If you choose carefully, the novelty of the item can compensate for the fact that it was inexpensive.

- Perform an unsolicited act of kindness

  Every city election day I send snacks to the poll workers who must work from before 7 AM until after 7 PM. They are an important part of the election process that is the hallmark of democracy in this country. Without these volunteers, the process would not work the way it does; yet they are often overlooked. So, I take time to deliver to them, snacks and drinks (including lots of chocolate) so they can have munchies throughout the day to keep their energy and their spirits up.

Homework

Keep a Gratitude Journal

Jot down, in the journal, those things for which you are grateful. Consider small things in each of the following categories and/or create additional categories of your own: concrete things, abstract things, things in nature, spiritual things. Be sure your journal has a focus on *people* who have touched your life in some way. For example, you might express gratitude to the safety officer at your child's school or the receptionist at an office you visit. Make a note in your journal reminding yourself to handwrite a thank you note letting them know how much you appreciate them. This gesture will not only make their day but it will make yours as well.

Establish a "gratitude bin/box"

Set aside a container in which you can put small items that come your way that can be gifted to people to express your gratitude. For example, you may have gotten some "freebies" at a conference you attended or a coupon or gift as a result of being a frequent shopper at a particular store. Always having

Perfection is the enemy of progress. Striving to be perfect leaves you unsatisfied; it keeps you from enjoying your journey. I used to chase perfection all of the time, stressing out about whether something was perfect. A remembrance that comes to mind is of the first time I took baked goods to my children's school for a bake sale – I burned the brownies. The stress was overwhelming; I went to the store and bought ingredients to make more. Then I struggled to cut them precisely and make them look perfect because I was so worried about being judged by other moms. I even scripted their imaginary feedback in my head: "Oh, look at Miss Busy Work Mom, doing this and that at the city, but she can't even find time to make brownies." Despite my efforts and the tremendous stress I created for myself, I never achieved the perfect brownies (although the second batch was okay and served my purpose). Ironically, my kids didn't really care that the product was not perfect; I had involved them in the baking process and *they*, at least, had fun! I share this story because I know many other mothers do what I was doing; they focus so much on what they think is perfect or on what they believe other people will think is perfect, that they forfeit the joy they could gain from countless experiences in their lives.

The predominant role of social media in our lives today can exacerbate the pursuit of perfection. We see others post information about their vacation experiences and whatever new possessions they have acquired. We compare our own experiences and acquisitions to theirs. We tell ourselves that we are not good enough or that what we have doesn't measure up to what they have. We intensify our pursuit of perfection only to be disappointed again by our inability to achieve that goal. We redouble our efforts and repeat the cycle of comparison, disappointment, and intensified pursuit of perfection. This vicious cycle threatens our physical and psychological health, prevents us from living in the moment, inhibits our ability to express thankfulness for what we do have and steals the joy from our lives.

Releasing a preoccupation with perfection – giving up the notion that you have to bake perfect brownies, have to have the perfect vacation, have to look perfect, have to engage daily in financially lucrative work and have to be super mom – does not mean abandoning your worthy goals. It does not mean not striving to be better and do better. It does mean ceasing the fruitless pursuit of an unattainable ideal. It does mean checking the tendency to submit to feelings of guilt because you have not achieved perfection. It does mean resisting the urge to compare yourself to others. It does mean acknowledging your worth, your worthiness and, as John Legend sings, "all your perfect imperfections."

There is not a week that goes by that I don't have someone asking me how I do it all. I used to say perfunctorily, "I don't think about it, I just do it." As I have reflected more deeply about a response to the question, I have begun to say, "I had to learn to let go of the desire to be perfect and just enjoy what is." My prayer for each woman reading this book, is that you learn to exist in the moment. Be happy with what you have; do your best and know that, even as you strive for excellence, your best is <u>enough</u>. Remind yourself that perfection, like work-life balance, is an unattainable goal. Neither perfection, nor work-life balance exist for us in any achievable way. However, excellence and work-life *integration* <u>are</u> achievable. Above all, remember that if you were perfect, you'd have wings!

Homework

Throw yourself a Perfectly Imperfect Party. Grab a glass of wine (or sparkling cider), set out a few munchies, gather a few girlfriends and celebrate the perfection of your imperfections.

RULE # 9

Identify the Right Village

When I had my children's baby dedications, I was instructed by my pastor – with reference to the adage, "it takes a village to raise a child" – to invite our village. The adage is accurate, but I challenge us to expand its scope by recognizing that the need for a village does not end with childhood. We each need a village to help and support us as we go through life. Your village need not be a large one; actually, a smaller one is probably best. However, your village does need to be a strong one, composed of people who will have your back when you really need them; people who are with you whether you are doing well or experiencing challenges; people who will be committed to you for who you are – flaws and all – not for your title, prestige, money or status.

Who are the members of *your* village? It is imperative that your village be comprised of the right people – people who will be there for you when others are not, people who are with you for the right reasons. My husband often says that people who are **with** you are not always *for* you. As you climb the ladder of success, you will encounter people who only want to be around you because of who you are and what you can do for them. Be wary of those people; they are unlikely to tell you the truth about situations and unlikely to be there when times are rough. People may *hang with* you and have fun with you; this doesn't mean they are meant to be in your village.

Pastor T.D. Jakes has one of the most inspiring and educational descriptions about friendship that I have ever heard. (It is on YouTube, so you can google it). In his sermon, Pastor Jakes discusses three categories of friends: confidants, constituents and comrades. He explains that *confidants* are those people in your life who love you unconditionally and will be there for you no matter what. This is the category I consider my "ride or die:" my mom, my husband and a handful of really great girlfriends (and a few guy friends). Confidants don't care about your money, status, titles, looks or lifestyle. They will also be honest with you when needed. They will tell you when you are wrong and refuse to let you do things that are self-sabotaging, even if you get angry at them. Confidants are the friends to whom you tell your dreams. They are the ones who support your dream, encourage your dream and respect your dream in ways that show that they love your dream because they love you. When you are happy, they're happy for you.

Constituents are friends who are with you and for you, but only for as long as you are for what they are for – in other words, only for as long as you can help them get what they want. Constituent friends are not confidants; If they meet someone whom they feel can do more for them than you can, they are willing to leave you for that person. Constituent friends remind me of the insecure mean girls in high school who will drop you for a more popular set of friends. If you mistake constituent friends for confidants, you risk being hurt.

Comrades are friends who are there for a season. Pastor Jakes analogizes them to scaffolding. They come in when something needs to be done, then leave when the job or task is over.

I love Pastor Jakes' explanations; when you know these categories, it is easier to decide who should be included in your village. It seems clear that your village should consist of confidants, but how do you distinguish one type of friend from another? Making the distinction is often difficult. You may, as I have, experience instances wherein people you think are confidants are revealed as comrades only. These experiences can be hurtful, for while your success can reveal your supporters, it can also expose your haters.

One strategy for determining who your confidant friends really are is to pay attention to how they react when you share your dreams or accomplishments with them. Do they hesitate? Do they seem less than enthused? Do they pick apart what you are saying or point out all the negatives in what you are sharing? If so, these individuals are not confidant material and should not be counted among the members of your village. These are individuals who will attempt to appropriate your dream for themselves or who may try to sabotage you. Often, they will begin to "hate" on you. The fact that these descriptions are probably familiar to most of us, suggests that when it comes to identifying worthy village members, "the struggle is real."

When determining who your village members are, it is natural to want to include people who have been where you've been or have been where you are – people who can relate to what you might be going through. Let's say, for example, that you are a non-profit owner working in the non-profit arena. Knowing that friends from that non-profit world would likely relate to you and the challenges you face (e.g., frustrations about grants) better than supportive and empathetic individuals with no experience in the non-profit sector, you would likely want to make sure that confidants from the non-profit world were part of your village. However, despite any inclination to confide in individuals who seem similar to you in significant ways (e.g., profession, experience, etc.) it is imperative that you identify village members whom you can trust.

Trustworthiness is one of the most essential attributes of your village members. For example, you should not assume that a work colleague (someone similar to you professionally) would be a suitable confidant, someone with whom you could share work issues you might be experiencing. If that individual is not trustworthy, s/he might tell your business to your supervisor or to others with whom you work. Members of your village must inspire your confidence that you can be "real" with them, that you can be yourself, that you can share honestly without fear of judgment or criticism.

Homework

- List the members of your village
- Indicate the role each member plays in your life, the lives of your children, the well being of your family (e.g., advisor, encourager, accountability coach, tutor, etc.).
- Specify what you/your family can do to nurture relationships with these village members.

RULE # 10

〰〰〰〰〰〰〰〰〰〰〰〰〰〰〰〰

Hire Your Weakness

The best CEOs are great because they know how to assemble a great team. Hiring someone or outsourcing a particular task can help you build what I like to call your *Dream Team*.

I once had a coach who regularly told us, "Hire your weakness..." and I wondered, "What does Coach mean?" What she meant, I eventually learned, was that if you are not adept at or efficient at a particular task, it might be worth your while to hire someone else to do it. In essence, the coach's advice refers to the wisdom of conducting a written or mental "cost-benefit analysis" that would inform you whether it is more economical to perform a task yourself or pay someone else to perform it. Your cost-benefit analysis should respond to questions such as: (a) *Am I good at this task?* (b) *How long would it take me to complete the task?* (c) *Do I have the time to complete the task?* (d) *How much is my time actually worth?* (e) *Is there someone who could accomplish the task with greater skill and efficiency* (e.g., in less time) *than I could?* Your responses to these questions would enable you to compare the "costs" versus the "benefits" of doing something yourself or employing another person to do it.

For example, I love to cook and I do a good job when I do cook. However, with my schedule, I don't always have time to cook. Too often I cannot get home and prepare a home-cooked meal by my children's scheduled bedtime; consequently, spending an hour in the kitchen after work is not cost-effective for me. As a result, I have looked for efficient ways to make sure that my family is fed, that they're fed something nutritious and that I have the time I need for other important things: attending community or PTO meetings, helping the children with homework, or just relaxing. One of the things I discovered last year is a meal prep service. There are several meal prep services available wherein you purchase a subscription and the service sends you a box each week that contains all of the ingredients you need for a meal(s). I love these services for many reasons:

1. They help you save time. You can prepare a meal in less than 30 minutes.
2. They help you save money; you don't have to buy meal ingredients in larger quantities than you need for a single meal.
3. They provide well-balanced meals.

4. They provide a variety of meals. Not only am I able to feed my children something healthy and nutritious, I'm able to expand their palates. When I cook on the regular basis, they're menu requests are very limited: spaghetti or meatloaf or tacos. However, these meal prep services enable me to present them with more varied options. They are able to try different things and say, "Oh yeah, I like that," or "Mom, I don't like that so much."

In addition to "hiring my weakness" with regard to meal preparation, I also hire my weakness with regard to housekeeping. Given my schedule, I do not have a lot of time to devote to house cleaning. I am not by nature a "messy" person, but three children – one of whom is a toddler – can render our house pretty messy at times. I try to schedule time for housekeeping first thing in the morning (e.g., around 5 AM) when everyone else is sleeping and the house is quiet. But even my early morning cleaning does not provide enough time to clean the house the way it needs to be cleaned. In addition, laundry, dishes and other critical family maintenance tasks require several hours per week.

In performing a cost-benefit analysis related to house cleaning, I considered the time I have available and how valuable my time is. For example, as an attorney, I bill at $200 an hour; as a coach, I average between $500 – $1000 per session. Given the monetary value of my time, it does not make sense for me to clean the house myself when I can hire a person or company to do it at a fraction of the time and cost. Therefore, I have hired someone who can help me. She excels at her job, enjoys the work and completes tasks in a fraction of the time that it would take me. Examples of other services that you can hire to help you utilize your time more efficiently include grocery shopping services, personal shopping services/stylist, kid taxi services and laundry services.

Hiring does not always mean you are paying someone to assist you; you can also obtain help in other ways. For example, an intern or protege can assist you with some of your business tasks or with things on your personal to-do list. Each summer I seek out an intern for my part-time job on the City Council. Actually, the job responsibilities are full time, but the stipend is part time – meaning that Council members are unable to hire staff to assist with all the tasks the position requires. The summer intern helps me with constituent communication and special projects. I typically have no trouble finding someone who wants to learn from the experience and for whom getting paid is not a priority. It is a win-win situation – the intern gains, I get much-needed assistance.

RULE # 11

Reclaim Your Time

O n many occasions in my life, I have been asked to help someone with a task – to do a favor. My almost-automatic response has been to agree to help. I recall a particular instance, however, when I began to rethink my tendency to always say, "yes" to requests. In this instance, a call came from an associate who needed my help with something. My response was, "Sure, I don't mind doing it." I rearranged my schedule in order to fulfill the request. The associate and I agreed to meet at a designated time so that I could transmit the requested information. Not only was my associate late for our appointment, but once there, did not seem to appreciate what I had done on his/her behalf. For example, the associate was unwilling to pay for the work. Actually, although I would normally have charged a client for the work, I had not intended to charge my associate. However, given that I had rearranged my schedule, devoted valuable time and expended a good deal of energy on the request, it rankled that the associate seemed to have no appreciation for my time, my effort or my skill.

After my meeting with the person, I thought to myself, "That was time I could have spent more gratifyingly: I could have been enjoying my family, building my business, relaxing, spending time with myself, getting a massage, etc." I was obliged to think deeply about what had happened and, although tempted to be angry at my associate, I realized that it was *I* who had *allowed* the individual to infringe upon my time. Honestly, I was rather angry at myself or, more accurately, *disappointed* in myself. How could I expect others to value my time if I didn't value it sufficiently to protect it from abuse? In the instance with my associate, I should have laid out very clear parameters regarding my input or cost (e.g., anticipated time, energy, skill, etc.), if I agreed to the request and what I expected in return (e.g., timely attendance at scheduled meetings). That associate helped me learn a valuable lesson.

Traditionally, women have been socialized to believe that placing a premium on their time and talent is selfish or self-centered. It is not! You must understand the value of your time and you must make sure that people with whom you work or interact also value your time. There will be some people who do not, for various reasons, appreciate or value things that are of value to you. That lack of appreciation is disrespectful of you and your time. Allowing people to take liberties with your time and talent, particularly when they are unappreciative, gives them something they do not really deserve – time that you could better spend with your family, friends, children. In other words, time spent with people who don't value your time, don't value your talents, don't appreciate what you have to offer, is time that is not available to spend with family and friends.

I mentioned, in an earlier chapter, that on my office desk, I have pictures of my family. These pictures do not face outward toward people who are in my office; they are turned toward me. Consequently, when I am facing someone who might be a drain on my time and my energy, someone who doesn't appreciate my time and my talents, I am also viewing the pictures of my loved ones. I can ask myself, "With whom would I rather spend time?" Ask yourself this question the next time you are faced with a time-drainer or energy-stealer, someone who wants something from you – your time, your talents, your advice, your opinions – but doesn't appreciate the time and energy you put into providing it. If your answer is that you would rather spend time with the ones you love, then you should emulate Maxine Waters and "reclaim" your time.

Build Multiple Streams of Income

Another way to reclaim your time is by building multiple streams of income. You should not be working so hard to make a living that you are not really living. Diversifying your income or having multiple income streams reduces your reliance on a single income source and prevents you from having to spend all of your time working.

Any good financial advisor will tell you that the number one rule for an investor is to build a diversified portfolio in order to reduce risk. Creating multiple income streams reduces risk in much the same way as a diversified investment portfolio: if one income source dries up, there are other sources exist to lessen the loss. I learned this lesson the hard way.

When I first started my law practice in 2001, I was primarily doing real estate closings. By 2005, my firm was doing very well. We had a growing staff to handle day-to-day operations and I was regularly bringing home over $10,000 a month. I was saving money, paying off debt and travelling. I was living the life, until.......THE HOUSING MARKET BUBBLE BURST and my business dried up. I went from having overflow and excess to barely being able to pay my bills. It was a huge blow to my wallet and to my self-esteem. However, I learned a very valuable lesson.... as my great-grandmother would say, "Never put all your eggs in one basket."

Luckily, my husband had a steady income and when the real estate market was good we had invested in real estate. Thus, when the housing market dropped, we had some resources on which to rely. However, I realized that, whether in my law firm or my household, it was unwise to rely on a single source of income. I immediately diversified the areas of my law practice and began to look for ways to diversify my household income as well, building a mixture of active and passive income. Presently, my law practice handles real estate, as well as probate and personal injury cases; I have an insurance license; I have a coaching certification and a blog; I am accepting speaking engagements; and I am building a book sales business. Additionally, my husband and I own several rental properties. If my law firm were my sole source of income, I would feel that I had to work there all of the time; I would still be stuck in the mindset, "If I am not working, I am not getting paid – so I need to work." Multiple streams of income have allowed me to reclaim my time and spend it the way I choose.

Numerous financial advisement sources have described strategies for creating varied income streams. Among the suggestions, for example, are to: (a) offer a service or sell something, (b) create a product, (c) start a blog, (d) write an ebook, (e) create an online course (f) identify something you love or love to do – your passion – and find ways to monetize it. Building multiple streams of income will allow you to make a life and enjoy it. To quote country singer and actress, Dolly Parton, "Don't get so busy making a living that you forget to make a life."

Homework

Before you can analyze how much it might cost you to perform "favors" for colleagues, acquaintances, even friends and family, you should have some idea of how much your time is worth. So, make that calculation:

1. Document your hourly value
   a. If you are paid wages, indicate how much you make per hour.
   b. If you receive a salary, compute your hourly rate.
   c. Adjust your figure, as needed, to account for the expertise or experience that tends to cause people to ask you for help in the first place. (Consider the "going rate" for the service you may be providing as a favor.)
2. If applicable, *guesstimate* the cost of materials you might use.
   a. For example, if you bake well and are constantly being asked for baked contributions, indicate how much you typically spend to prepare a given baked good.

3. Use these figures to place a "value" on your time.

Then, when considering whether to say "yes" to a particular request, think about (a) how much your time would be worth; (b) whether you actually *have* the time, given other responsibilities; (c) your relationship to the requester; and (d) whether the requester is prone to be an "energy drain" or unappreciative. If you keep these considerations in mind, you can decide with integrity, with respect for yourself and with acceptance of full responsibility for the outcome of your decision.

RULE # 12

◇◇◇◇◇◇◇◇◇◇◇◇◇◇◇◇◇◇◇◇◇◇◇◇◇◇

Build a Legacy

I had a work-related trip to Atlanta and used that opportunity to practice "work-life integration" by making a mini family vacation out of the trip. I go to Atlanta frequently, but never really experienced it like a tourist until recently. During this trip, we took the family to the World of Coca-Cola, an Atlanta museum that show-cases the history of The Coca-Cola Company.

During the visit, we learned that Coca-Cola was created by an Atlanta pharmacist named Dr. John S. Pemberton. Dr. Pemberton created a flavored syrup, which he mixed with carbonated water thus creating the cola that would become the world's #1 sparkling beverage. The Coca-Cola Company, which started with one cola that sold for 5 cents a glass, is now a global brand with a variety of beverages, including soda, water, juice and energy drinks. Although Dr Pemberton died a few years after he created the company and never got to see what it turned into, his legacy lives on.

Starting the Coca-Cola company was not building a career, it was building a legacy.

A legacy emerges from how you live your life and how what you do impacts the larger world. What will be your legacy? How are you making people's lives better? At the later days of your life will you look back and say I had an amazing career, but I was never home for my family. Or will you look back and say I could have been a great _____ (fill in the blank) but .....

Children are an obvious legacy: raising smart, independent and caring children who will grow up to love themselves, love others and contribute positively to the community is a great legacy.

We all have a finite amount of time and energy. We often get so busy with the hustle and bustle of our everyday lives that we get distracted from the true legacy we are building and settle for ordinary.

When I started The Possibilities Institute in 2014 I wanted not only to create a business that would allow me to get paid for my skills and talents, but I wanted also to help other women create their legacies. That is why the mission of the Institute is to help women leaders and moms to discover their leadership possibilities, maximize their potential and *live a life that leaves a legacy.* As I work with my clients, I challenge them to think bigger than themselves. I challenge them understand that they are building their legacy with each new experience, every personal interaction and every deposit they make into improving the life of someone else. I help them create their personal and professional action plans knowing that we are also creating a blueprint for the legacy they want to leave.

At the end of my life, I want to be able to look back and see that I had an amazing life. I want to say that I had an amazing career and was able to enjoy the fruits of my labor. I want to say that I travelled to amazing places, met awesome people and raised amazing children who will be leaders in this world. I want to say that I loved and was loved. I want a legacy that includes changing the narrative that women have to sacrifice a successful career to raise a family. I want a legacy that includes lasting memories of family time, special experiences and contributions to the community. I want my life to leave a legacy that evokes pride in my children and my children's children. What will be your legacy?

Summary

In this book I have translated principles used by successful company CEOs into 12 rules that women can apply to their personal life in order to achieve the work-life integration for which so many of us yearn. These rules are as follows:

1. Operate as the CEO of your life.
2. Identify and monitor the big "why?" of your life.
3. Organize the content of your life.

4. Create memories.

5. Create a bucket list.

6. Deal with "Mom guilt."

7. Express gratitude.

8. Eliminate an obsession with perfection.

9. Identify the right "village."

10. Hire your weakness.

11. Reclaim your time.

12. Build a legacy.

If you apply these rules with diligence, you will manage your life in a way that keeps your priorities in order; you will implement strategies that help you operate at peak performance; and you will create the freedom, flexibility and success that enables you to live the life you desire.

I would love to hear how you apply these principles and how they work on your journey to better work life integration. Please visit our website at www. possibilitiesinstitute.com and send me an email or share some of your work life integration successes.

Testimonials

Tameika Isaac Devine is a leading voice for the empowerment of working women. Her life experience offers insight into techniques useful for today's busy women, who seek a healthy balance between career, family and community.

~ Rachel Hodges,
Former First Lady of SC and
mother of two sons.

. . . .

If you have felt the frustration of feeling like you should be able to balance your work and your life, yet you have failed time and time again at accomplishing this task, then your search is over! Tameika Isaac Devine smashes the myth of balance and brings you deep insight into the world of integration. So, put your "Wonder Woman" t-shirt in the closet and get ready to learn how to live an integrated life! This book is the first step on your journey!

~ Dr. Katrina Eichelberger
-Hutchins (Dr. K) President & CEO, Re-Source
Solutions. Mother of two and grandmother of two

. . . .

Throw out the tired approach of life balance! Instead, apply Tameika's approach of determining your priorities and integrating them into one life...yours. This brief but insightful book provides a step-by-step approach to combine work, family, and leisure into one satisfying, enjoyable and productive life.

~ Anne Sinclair,
Partner, Resource Associates, Inc.
& Former Councilwoman,
City of Columbia, Mother of three

. . . .

*We're all **good** at being mothers, managers and community leaders...but through her personal story and solid examples Tameika shows us how to be **great** at it! She gives us permission to own our weaknesses and use our strengths to truly create an integrated life plan that benefits our communities, our work teams and most importantly – our families.*

~ Lila Anna Sauls,
President & CEO of Homeless No More.
Commissioner, Richland One Board of School
Commissioners. Mom of five.

. . . .

Tameika is a proven leader and great wife and mother and appears to do it effortlessly. In this new book, Tameika shares her approach to work life integration and shows us that we all feel we fall short sometimes, including her. But that instead of trying to live up to unrealistic expectations, you can truly have an amazing life filled with abundant blessings without stress, guilt or overwhelm, its all in the approach and the way you look at it. Think Like A CEO, Act Like A Mom is a must read for all women out there feeling like they can "balance" it all so help to on the path of true work life integration.

~ Mia McLeod,
State Senator, State of South Carolina and President/CEO of McLeod Butler. Mother of two

· ·

As wives, mothers, daughters, professionals and community leaders, we juggle a lot of things. The day-to-day demands on us from the different segments of our lives can cause us to feel like we're swimming upstream at times. This amazing book teaches us the power of saying no and aligning our priorities with impactful goals without feeling guilty. This candid book demystifies being a working mom with high professional goal. Tameika shows us that being authentically and unapologetically yourself is the best real example you can give the world and by showing up that way, you, your family and community will be better for it.

~ Mayor Deana Holiday Ingraham,
Mayor of East Point, GA and Attorney.
Mother of one.

· ·

Tameika Isaac Devine is the epitome of a true work-life balance strategist. She not only talks her talk, but she is walking and living her best life every day. Tameika shows women in the work force that the goal of life is not perfection, but about embracing the possibilities and going after them. She shows you step by step how she, through believing in her dreams, and mapping out a sound strategy achieved her dreams, and how you can too.

~ Dr. Colleen Hawthorne, M.D.
C-Suite Concierge Psychiatric Medical Doctor
and Vibrant Life Success Confidant,
Consultant and Coach.
www.DrColleenHawthorne.com

. . . .

About The Author

Wife, mother, practicing attorney, elected official, entrepreneur, professional speaker, best-selling author and certified personal and executive coach, Tameika Isaac Devine is one of the nation's leading experts on work-life integration. As the Founder of **The Possibilities Institute**, she works with women leaders and mothers to empower them to discover their leadership possibility, maximize their potential and live a life that leaves a legacy. She is a strong believer that women can have happy and fulfilling personal lives without sacrificing their professional goals and aspirations. She works with dozens of women to help them achieve work-life integration so that they can have amazing careers without feeling guilty or overwhelmed.

At age 29, Mrs. Devine made history when she was first elected as a member of the Columbia, SC City Council, becoming the **first** African American female elected to the City Council and the first African American to be elected at-large. She is in her 5th term on the Council and is currently serving as Mayor Pro Tem.

Mrs. Devine is a frequent guest on radio: *The Urban Scene* with Don Frierson, *In Touch* with Judi Gatson, WIS News, WLTX and WACH Fox 57 News. She has also appeared on MSNBC, CNN and NPR.

Mrs. Devine is one half of a dynamic couple. She is married to Jamie L. Devine, a member of the Richland One Board of School Commissioners. Although, the Devines continue to be very busy in the community, their priority is being parents to their 3 children: Tamia, Jade and Jameson. They are also the parents to a beautiful angel baby, James Henry, who was born into heaven on August 28, 2014.